AEI LEGISLATIVE ANALYSES
*Balanced analyses of current proposals before the Congress, prepared
with the help of specialists in law, economics, and government.*

Reform of Social Security and Federal Pension Cost-of-Living Adjustments

1985
99th Congress
1st Session

AMERICAN ENTERPRISE INSTITUTE
FOR PUBLIC POLICY RESEARCH
Washington, D.C.

To order call toll free 1-800-462-6420 or 1-717-794-3800. For all other inquiries please contact the AEI Press, 1150 Seventeenth Street, N.W., Washington, D.C. 20036 or call 1-800-862-5801.

ISBN 978-0-8447-0264-3
Legislative Analysis No. 49, 99th Congress
July 1985

CONTENTS

1
INTRODUCTION

Inflation, by reducing the purchasing power of a dollar, harms those whose incomes are fixed in nominal terms. To protect the elderly from economic hardship due to the erosion of their real benefits, Congress indexed social security benefits to the cost of living as measured by the consumer price index (CPI). The pensions of railroad retirees, civil service workers, military personnel, and disabled coal miners are also indexed. These cost-of-living adjustments (COLAs) have protected the real benefits of recipients over a period of rapid inflation in the past ten years. The federal government has been able to provide beneficiaries with full inflation protection because of its ability to use tax revenues to fund COLAs. In the private sector, where pensions must be funded from contributions, such protection is limited because of the expense and uncertainty it entails for pension plans.

Attention has focused on reform of the COLAs for two reasons. First, there is widespread agreement that the necessary federal budget deficit reduction should rely on budget cuts rather than tax increases. Social security benefits account for a large portion of domestic program outlays, and an effort to share the burden of deficit reduction has naturally focused attention on them. A temporary reduction in the COLA payments for social security and the other programs listed above is viewed by some as a less painful way to achieve budget reductions because it entails no reduction in current benefits but lowers or temporarily halts the increase in those benefits. The administration proposal modifies the COLA formula temporarily and increases benefits under the Supplemental Security Income (SSI) program to mitigate the effect of the COLA reduction on the elderly poor.

The second reason attention has focused on social security COLAs is that they may cause long-term problems. One possible problem arises because indexed major federal expenditures would automatically increase outlays and could make the budget difficult to control (or more difficult than in the absence of COLAs). Another long-term problem concerns the long-run financing of social security. In the late 1970s, the United States experienced a fall in labor productivity, which led to a situation in which prices rose more rapidly than wages. Since social security benefits are normally indexed to prices and the taxes that finance them are based on

1

wages, this kind of situation, if it were to occur again, could lead to financing problems for the social security system. As a result of this experience, the COLA structure has been modified in an effort to protect the financial integrity of the system if such a situation recurs.

This legislative analysis examines the arguments for and against reducing the COLAs for social security and other federal retirement and disability programs, with particular attention to the administration proposal and the policy that was passed by the Senate in May 1985. The history of indexation of social security and other federal programs is reviewed, and alternative proposals for altering COLAs will be discussed.

2

BACKGROUND

Outlays for many federal programs rise with overall inflation or with the increase in specific prices related to the program. Some programs' outlays increase because of direct ties either to the consumer price index or to other price (or wage) indexes, other programs' outlays because the cost of the goods or services they purchase increases.[1] This analysis focuses entirely on programs directly linked to the CPI, specifically on those providing benefits to retired or disabled workers.[2] The major programs in this category (in terms of expenditures) are Old Age, Survivors and Disability Insurance (OASDI), railroad retirement, Supplemental Security Income, civil service retirement, and military retirement.[3] The history and current status of indexation for these programs are discussed below, starting with OASDI, which accounts for the largest budget outlays.[4]

INDEXATION OF SOCIAL SECURITY

The 1972 Social Security Amendments. On June 30, 1972, both houses of Congress passed a bill to extend the public debt limit. Attached to this bill were amendments to the Social Security Act instituting automatic adjustments of benefits in response to future increases in the CPI. This COLA provision was to be financed by automatic increases in the contribution and benefit base. The next day, President Richard Nixon signed the bill into law (P.L. 92-336).[5]

The indexation scheme was to start operating in 1974. In that year the rate of change of the CPI between the third quarter of 1972 and the second quarter of 1974 was used to determine the COLA payment to be paid in July 1975. In subsequent years the procedure would use the rate of change of the CPI between the second quarter of the year and either the second quarter of the year in which the last COLA was effective or the last quarter in which a general benefit increase was made effective. If the calculated rate of increase was greater than or equal to 3 percent, an automatic benefit increase would be effective on January 1 of the following year.[6]

As noted above, P.L. 92-336 also included provisions for financing the COLA through automatic escalation of the earnings base for contribution and benefit purposes. The base is raised only in years when a COLA

3

has been granted for cash benefits. The procedure used is to multiply the base by the ratio of average taxable wages in the first quarter of the year of determination to average taxable wages in the first quarter of the year in which the last base increase was enacted. The result is rounded to the nearest $300. This, if it does not constitute a reduction of the base, gives the new base effective the next year.[7]

In October 1972 P.L. 92-603, which included additional amendments to the Social Security Act, was passed. It provided for the indexation of the earnings test—the maximum amount that can be earned (by recipients under seventy-two) without a reduction in benefits. The maximum amount was to be tied to increases in average earnings. These adjustments occur only when a COLA has been given for benefits. The procedure for adjustment is similar to that used to index the base.[8]

The first cost-of-living adjustment to benefits was effective in June 1975 and was paid in July of that year.[9] At that time benefits were raised 8 percent. Subsequent increases, effective in June 1976 and June 1977, were 6.4 percent and 5.9 percent respectively.[10]

The 1977 Social Security Amendments. In 1977 the Social Security Act was again amended. The amendments were proposed in response to both short-term and long-term financing problems for social security. The short-term problem was largely the result of the recession, but unexpectedly high inflation coupled with the COLA contributed to it. The long-term problem reflected the forecast of adverse demographic trends as well as difficulties due to inflation.[11] In particular, a technical flaw in the 1972 law led to an overindexation of benefits for workers who had not yet retired. This meant that outlay forecasts were heavily dependent on inflation forecasts and also implied that in certain situations workers could have replacement rates (the ratio of benefits to preretirement earnings) greater than 100 percent.[12]

The overindexation occurred because the procedure specified in the 1972 law adjusted future benefits (for current workers) twice for inflation.[13] Briefly, an increase in the CPI (greater than or equal to 3 percent) would lead to a proportionate increase in the benefit rate—the percentage of the person's average monthly wage that is given as a benefit.[14] This provision allows retirees' benefits to keep pace with the CPI. For workers who have not yet retired, inflation raises their future benefits through the COLA in a similar manner, but it also operates through a second channel. Generally, wages rise along with prices, so that a worker's average monthly earnings (AME) rise. Thus at retirement the higher benefit rate is applied to a higher AME, and the worker's benefits are overindexed. Under this system the replacement rate—benefits divided by earnings just before retirement—would increase over time. Since this effect accumulates over time, it is possible, even with moderate rates of inflation, to find eventual

4

replacement rates above 100 percent.[15]

As noted above, inflation contributed to both the short-term and the long-term financing problems. The difficulties became apparent quite quickly because of the historically high rates of inflation in the period beginning in 1973. The 1977 amendments revised the benefit structure to stabilize replacement rates.[16] Replacement rates were stabilized at 5 percent below the levels projected for 1979 under the prior structure.[17]

Under the 1977 amendments, benefits of retirees were indexed as specified in the 1972 amendments, but the calculation of the initial benefit amount for workers retiring after 1979 was changed to prevent progressive increases in the replacement rate. This change, usually referred to as decoupling, was called "the most significant amendment" and was estimated to have "eliminated about one-half of the future deficits" according to A. Haeworth Robertson, the chief actuary of social security at the time.[18]

The 1983 Social Security Amendments. Despite the 1977 amendments, the social security system continued to be plagued by both short-term and long-term financing problems. In 1983 the short-term problem was so severe that there was a possibility that benefits could not be paid on time in the second half of the year.[19] The severity of the problem reflected a worse aggregate economic performance than had been forecast in 1977.[20]

In response to the system's problems, President Ronald Reagan established the National Commission on Social Security Reform (NCSSR) in December 1981.[21] The final report of the commission reached the president and Congress in January 1983. It included two recommendations related to the COLA payments: (1) delay the 1983 COLA and shift future COLAs to a calendar-year basis (and increase the amount of social security benefits disregarded for SSI purposes); and (2) after 1987, if trust funds fall below 20 percent of outgo, base the COLA on the lower of price or wage increases (and include a provision for catch-up if funds exceed 32 percent of outgo).[22] In January 1983 President Reagan urged Congress to adopt the NCSSR proposal.[23] On April 20 the Social Security Amendments of 1983 became law (P.L. 98-21).[24]

The 1983 amendments included several provisions related to cost-of-living adjustments that were based on the NCSSR plan. The July 1983 COLA was delayed six months, until January 1984. All future COLAs were to be put on a calendar-year basis and to be paid in January rather than July. They were to be based on a third-quarter-to-third-quarter calculation of changes in the CPI. COLA increases in SSI and the Medicare premium were also placed on a calendar-year basis, and the July 1983 increase was delayed to January 1984. In July 1983 the SSI payment standard was increased by $20 per month for individuals and $30 per month for couples. In addition, a "stabilizer" was included, as suggested by the NCSSR.

5

Starting with the benefit increase payable in January 1985, COLA increases would be limited to the lesser of the increase in the CPI or the increase in wages *if* the ratio of the combined OASDI trust fund assets to estimated outgo fell below 15 percent. After 1988 a ratio of 20 percent will trigger the stabilizer. Wages are to be measured as they now are for the contribution and benefit base calculations. Finally, the law allows for a catch-up in cases where wage increases are used. The catch-up increases would occur when the trust fund ratio reached 32 percent and would use funds available above the 32 percent ratio. The benefits would then, if possible, be brought to the level they would have reached if the COLA had been based on price increases.

The Social Security Administration estimated at the time that the six-month delay of the COLA payment would reduce expenditures by $39.4 billion over the 1983–1989 period.[25] The stabilizer provision was not expected to be triggered, and no savings from this source were forecast.

INDEXATION OF CIVIL SERVICE PENSIONS

Automatic cost-of-living adjustments for civil service annuities were established in P.L. 87-793, enacted in 1962. This law provided an automatic COLA when the increase in the CPI in the base year exceeded 3 percent. The percentage increase in benefits was to equal the increase in the CPI and be effective on April 1 of the following year. Those retired less than one year were not eligible for the COLA.[26]

The COLA was revised in 1965. The increase in the CPI that triggered the COLA was changed from an annual to a monthly basis. Specifically, a COLA was triggered whenever the CPI rose by at least 3 percent from the month on which the last COLA was based and remained at or above 3 percent for three consecutive months. When this occurred, the COLA would equal the highest monthly increase during those three months. This change was made to allow for faster and more frequent adjustments than under the 1962 law. This law also removed the one-year retirement requirement to receive COLAs.[27]

In October 1969 the COLA formula was amended to compensate retirees for the five-month period between the first increase of 3 percent and the date on which the COLA payment was made. To do this, P.L. 91-93 provided for a 1 percent add-on to all COLA payments.[28]

In the late 1960s it became apparent that the removal of the requirement of one year's retirement to receive the COLA (specified in the 1965 law) was creating a serious problem. Since all annuities payable on the effective date of the COLA were increased, there was an incentive for people to retire the day before a COLA was effective. For employees whose pay rates were frozen remaining on the job implied lower retirement bene-

6

fits. Since this effect was cumulative, it provided a significant incentive for those workers to retire. This problem was corrected in 1973 by a change in the procedure for calculating the initial annuity amount.[29]

The COLA computation was changed again in 1976 in response to what many believed was an overcompensation for inflation due to the 1 percent add-on. The add-on was repealed, and to compensate the COLA payments were moved from an annual to a semiannual basis with no trigger percentage. Benefits were to be adjusted each March and September no matter how small the percentage change in the CPI. In 1980 COLA payments for recent retirees were prorated—the annuitant receives one-sixth of the COLA for each month in retirement status since the last adjustment.[30]

The Omnibus Budget Reconciliation Act of 1981 returned COLA payments to an annual basis and based them on the December-to-December change in the CPI, to be effective in March. Thus no COLA was given in September 1981. In 1982 the Omnibus Budget Reconciliation Act of 1982 delayed the COLAs one month in each of the years 1983 to 1985.[31] This change also applied to the military retirement system and the Foreign Service retirement system.

Finally, the Omnibus Budget Reconciliation Act of 1983 eliminated the May 1984 and June 1985 COLAs and replaced them with a COLA payment effective in December 1984 and payable in January 1985. Future COLAs were to be annual and based on the third-quarter-to-third quarter CPI change.[32]

OTHER FEDERAL RETIREMENT AND DISABILITY PROGRAMS

Railroad Retirement. The Railroad Retirement System provides what are essentially social security benefits for railroad workers (tier I benefits) as well as a private-employer-financed pension (tier II benefits). P.L. 93-445, passed in 1974 and effective in 1976, indexed tier I benefits to social security benefits and tier II benefits to increases in the CPI. The initial portion of the tier II benefit increases by 65 percent of the rise in the CPI, and the other portion rises by 32.5 percent of the CPI increase. The tier II COLAs were effective in 1977. All COLAs are paid annually.[33]

Other Social Security–Linked Programs. The Supplemental Security Income program is a means-tested federal program for the aged, blind, and disabled that began in 1974. Benefit increases are tied to those given for social security benefits. The adjustment and timing of the COLAs are identical with those in the social security program. Veterans' pensions and survivor benefits are similarly tied to social security benefits.[34]

7

The Military Retirement System and Other Federal Retirement Systems. Military retirement benefits were first indexed to the CPI in 1963.[35] Since then several revisions have been made, so that the COLA formula is now the same as that of the federal civil service retirement system. Other federal retirement programs using this formula include the Foreign Service retirement system, the Federal Reserve Board retirement system, the Comptroller General's retirement system, and the retirement systems of the Central Intelligence Agency and the Tennessee Valley Authority.[36]

3
LEGISLATIVE PROPOSALS CONCERNING COLA PAYMENTS

In his fiscal 1986 budget President Reagan proposed a one-year freeze of the cost-of-living adjustments for civil service and military retirees as well as a freeze in the COLA for tier II railroad retirement benefits. That is, he proposed eliminating the January 1986 COLA payments for these programs. The administration also proposed a change in the civil service COLA computation, which would limit the COLA to the lesser of the CPI increase or the federal white-collar pay increase and the COLA for retirees with benefits above $10,000 to 55 percent of the regular COLA.[37]

A compromise proposal worked out by the White House and the Senate Republican leadership was introduced in the Senate in April. This proposal called for limiting COLAs for all non-means-tested retirement and disability programs to 2 percent plus the excess of actual inflation over 4 percent.[38] The plan did not call for reductions in the COLAs for the SSI or food stamps programs but did propose raising SSI benefits by $10 per month for individuals and $15 per month for couples.[39] It was estimated by the Office of Management and Budget that the change in the social security COLA would save $3 billion in fiscal 1986 and $22.7 billion over the 1986–1988 period. Other COLA changes and civil service retirement reform would bring the total savings to $34 billion over the 1986–1988 period.[40]

In May the first concurrent budget resolutions passed by the Senate (S. Con. Res. 32) and the House (H. Con. Res. 152) proposed opposing policies with respect to the COLAs in non-means-tested programs. The Senate resolution would freeze the COLAs for social security, civilian and military retirement, and veterans' and other retirement programs in fiscal 1986. It also included SSI benefit increases of $10 per month for individuals and $15 per month for couples.[41] The House resolution provides full COLAs for all these programs.[42] The House Budget Committee estimates that the one-year freeze would save $7.4 billion in fiscal 1986 and $28 billion over the 1986–1988 period.[43]

4
ISSUES AND ARGUMENTS

In discussions of the pros and cons of freezing or reducing the 1986 COLA payments for social security and other federal retirement and disability programs, several key issues emerge. The first is whether social security, a self-financing program, should be part of an effort to reduce the overall budget deficit or should be considered independent of the rest of the federal budget. The other retirement programs present less of an issue because they rely on general revenue financing (as well as employee contributions in some cases).

If one believes that social security and the other programs are potential candidates for benefit cuts to help reduce the general budget deficit, then the issue of how they should be cut arises next, that is, whether the COLAs should be frozen or reduced. Opponents raise concerns about the effect of cuts on the income of the elderly and worry that they will increase the number of poor by reducing the purchasing power of benefits. An additional question is whether beneficiaries have been promised (are entitled to) a certain level of real benefits. The concern about the effects of a COLA freeze on the well-being of the aged leads some to seek alternative COLA reduction policies that would limit the effect on the aged poor. (This issue is addressed in the second section following.)

For the civil service, military, and other federal pension programs, the issue of increasing poverty among the aged is less relevant because far fewer of these beneficiaries are poor or near poor.[44] Here the issue of generosity is more relevant. Private sector pensions do not provide 100 percent inflation protection, and some critics believe that this protection for federal retirees is an unfair burden on taxpayers.

The final issue to be discussed is that of equity among beneficiaries. COLA reductions or freezes may lead to inequities among beneficiaries who retire in different years.

SOCIAL SECURITY AND THE UNIFIED BUDGET

Should social security be reduced in an effort to reduce the federal budget deficit? This question is related to a broader issue: Should social security be viewed as an integral part of the federal budget, or should it be treated

10

separately? In the past, changes in social security benefits (and taxes) were discussed in the specific context of the social security system. For example, the six-month COLA delay in the 1983 amendments was instituted in response to short-term financing problems of the social security system.[45] Should this perspective be changed?

There are several arguments in favor of a changed perspective. First, the potential budget savings from a COLA freeze are substantial. The Congressional Budget Office (CBO) estimates savings of $6.5 billion in fiscal 1986 if COLAs in all non-means-tested programs are eliminated. Over the 1986–1990 period, the total savings from a one-year freeze are estimated at $43.3 billion.[46] The magnitude of the savings makes this policy attractive as a deficit-reducing measure. In addition, this policy may be easier for recipients to accept than other potential cuts because it does not reduce nominal benefits but rather cuts the expected increase in benefits. Inflation then reduces the purchasing power, or real benefits. For those interested in spreading the burden of deficit reduction more broadly across the population, this policy will also appear attractive.

The issue that must still be addressed is whether social security benefits should be treated as an integral part of the budget. Cutting such benefits has the same effect on the budget deficit as other expenditure cuts. Since 1969 social security has been part of the unified budget, and a $1 cut in these benefits leads to a $1 reduction in the budget deficit. Confusion arises because a reduction in social security benefits, other things being equal, increases the balance in the social security trust funds rather than reduces the national debt. The funds in the social security trust funds are invested, however, in federal government securities. Most of these funds are invested in special issues of federal debt designed specifically for the trust funds. Although the trust funds do receive interest from the general account, this is merely an intragovernment transfer.[47] Thus, when social security benefits are reduced, the amount of public debt held outside the government is reduced, as it would be with other non-social-security outlay cuts. In other words, the amount of government securities that must be sold on the open market would be reduced, and the effect on financial markets and interest rates would be the same as for any similar change in budget outlays. The technical difference between social security benefits and other expenditures would matter only in a situation where the public debt ceiling was binding. In sum, for the advantages of deficit reduction, that is, lower interest rates, social security reductions are no different from other cuts.

It should be noted, however, that social security benefits are transfer payments to individuals rather than expenditures on goods and services. Therefore, cuts in those benefits constitute a less than 100 percent reduction in the aggregate demand for goods and services, since a $100 reduction in transfer payments generally reduces household demand not by $100 but by a smaller amount as households attempt to maintain their standard of living by saving less. In contrast, a reduction of $100 in expenditures on light bulbs is a $100 reduction in demand. In the short term, this implies that the negative economic effect is the same as for other transfers, that is, less than for reductions in expenditures on goods and services.

Another reason for including social security in the unified budget is to guarantee that it is subject to continuing fiscal review. The unified budget shows the economic effect of the federal government more accurately than a budget excluding social security. Since social security surpluses or deficits have effects similar to those of other budget surpluses or deficits, they should be taken into account in formulating fiscal policy. This is more easily done if they are included in a unified budget.

On the other side of the issue are many supporters of removing the social security system from the unified budget, among them the NCSSR. The NCSSR recommended that changes in social security be made for programmatic reasons only and not as part of an effort to balance the federal budget. In accordance, it recommended that social security be removed from the unified budget.[48] The 1983 Social Security Amendments provided for the removal of the operations of the trust funds from the unified budget in fiscal year 1993.[49]

The view of social security as separate from the rest of the budget arises because it is a self-financing program. Its benefits are paid from payroll taxes levied solely for this purpose. The payroll tax revenues cannot under current law be used directly for other purposes. Consequently, a reduction in COLA payments leads to an unplanned buildup of the trust funds. The trust funds are now running surpluses and are expected to continue in surplus until 2020,[50] and such COLA reductions lead to additional surpluses. Supporters of this view, then, argue that although the trust fund deficit or surplus (whether in or out of the unified budget) has the same economic effects as other elements of the deficit, it should be viewed as a separate entity for policy purposes. This implies that fiscal policy should take the social security trust fund balance as a given rather than as a potential tool.

An additional reason for this view is that since the payroll tax and the income tax are not integrated, the outlays should also be considered separately.[51] The social security payroll tax is more regressive than the federal income tax. (In other words, it collects a relatively larger percentage of income than the income tax as the individual's income falls.) For married workers (whose spouses have no income) whose wages are half the national average, social security taxes are greater than income taxes. As wages increase, the ratio of income taxes to social security taxes rises.[52] It might thus be reasonable to argue that unplanned surpluses in the trust funds should be used for payroll tax relief. Payroll tax rates are currently 7.05 percent for employees and are scheduled to rise to 7.65 percent in 1990.[53]

Some argue that using the social security system in a way that was not initially intended will undermine public faith in the system and heighten anxieties among the beneficiaries. More frequently, however, opponents of COLA freezes raise the issue of the adequacy of social security benefits and the effect of a reduction in real benefits on the well-being of the elderly.

COLA REDUCTIONS AND THE WELL-BEING OF THE AGED

The fact that social security benefits constitute over one-fifth of federal spending not only reflects their importance as a component of the federal budget but also suggests their significance as a source of income for the elderly. In 1982 benefits were received by 36.5 million people and provided close to 40 percent of the total income of the aged population.[54] Outlays for other federal retirement programs are about 30 percent of social security outlays.[55] Opponents of a COLA freeze point to the significant effect it may have on the economic well-being of the elderly. In attempting to gauge the effect of this policy on the aged, several issues must be addressed. First, it is useful to look at the economic position of the elderly in relation to the rest of the population and how it has changed over the recent past. Second, the extent of poverty among the aged and how it will be affected by the proposed policy should be discussed. In addition, it is useful to describe the cost of the delay of the July 1983 COLA for recipients and to examine the extent to which COLAs have compensated (or overcompensated) recipients for recent changes in the cost of living. This subsection focuses primarily on social security beneficiaries; the next subsection deals with the other retirement programs.

The Economic Situation of the Elderly. There is little doubt that the elderly are far better off today than they were twenty-five years ago and that a large part of the improvement in their economic welfare is due to the social security system. The mean real income of elderly families rose 45 percent from 1960 to 1983 despite a decline in labor force participation and an increase in the percentage of the elderly working part-time.[56] Much of this real income improvement is due to the increases in social security benefits, and some is due to the wider private pension coverage and greater pension benefits. Since 1970 real social security benefits have increased 46 percent on the average while real wages and salaries have fallen 7 percent. In addition, the fraction of the elderly receiving benefits has increased from 86 percent to 94 percent.[57]

On the basis of average income figures, elderly families appear to be on a par with the nonelderly. In 1983 per capita real income for elderly families was $9,080, and that for nonelderly families was $8,960.[58] There are,

13

however, reasons to suggest that this may not accurately portray the relative position of elderly families. First, the CPI, which is used to deflate the income figures, may not be as good a measure of the cost of living for the elderly as for the nonelderly. Since more elderly people own their own homes, for example, their expenses for homeownership are lower, and use of the CPI may understate their position in relation to the nonelderly. In addition, in deciding to retire, the elderly have chosen to consume more leisure at the expense of income, and this benefit is not included in the measure. The elderly consume more than the average amount of medical services, however. Since medical prices have risen faster than the average price level, use of the CPI may overstate the relative well-being of the elderly. It should also be noted that 1983 was a year of relatively high unemployment, which lowers the real income of the nonelderly more than that of the elderly.

Although these figures present a fairly rosy picture of the economic condition of the aged, it should be kept in mind that elderly widows are far worse off than elderly families. The mean real income of unrelated elderly individuals was only 60 percent of that of nonelderly unrelated individuals in 1983.[59]

These income comparisons are based on before-tax income, and this also leads to an understatement of the relative position of the aged. The elderly pay less tax on the average than the nonelderly because at least one-half of social security benefits is nontaxable and the elderly receive an additional $1,000 personal exemption from income taxes. In fact, the majority of elderly people pay no federal income tax.[60] An additional reason why the figures underestimate the relative status of the elderly is because they omit in-kind benefits, such as the care provided under the Medicare program.

In sum, a reasonable assessment of the situation is that the elderly are far better off now than twenty years ago and that a good deal of this improvement is due to the social security system (both old age and survivors' benefits and Medicare). The improvement in their economic situation does not imply that the benefits responsible for the improvement should be cut, but it does indicate that such a cut may not create significant hardship. One way to assess the hardship would be to focus on the poor and the near poor among the elderly who are social security recipients or recipients of other federal retirement programs.

Poverty among the Aged. As would be expected from the income figures above, the percentage of elderly families living in poverty has declined significantly over the past twenty-five years, from 27 percent in 1960 to 9 percent in 1983 (less than the 12 percent poverty rate for the nonelderly). For unrelated individuals over sixty-five, the poverty rate declined from 66 percent in 1960 to 26 percent in 1983. (The corresponding rate for the nonelderly was 18 percent.) The higher figure for unrelated individuals reflects the low income of elderly widows.[61]

On the basis of data from the March 1984 Current Population Survey, the Congressional Budget Office estimated that 3.9 million households receiving social security or railroad retirement benefits were below the poverty line in 1983.[62] Only 60,000 units receiving civil service or military retirement benefits had income below the poverty line. This implies a poverty rate of 17 percent for social security and railroad retirees and 2 percent for civil service and military retirees. The number of near poor households (between 100 and 125 percent of the poverty line) was 2.2 million for beneficiaries of the social security and railroad retirement programs and 90,000 for civil service and military retirees. The Supplemental Security Income program naturally has a poorer recipient population. Of 3 million beneficiary units in 1983, 1.6 million were poor, and 470,000 were near poor.[63]

According to CBO estimates, freezing the COLAs for all non-means-tested programs would, on average, reduce the income of poor elderly households by $130, approximately 3 percent of annual income. The elderly near poor would suffer an average loss of $180 (also about 3 percent of annual income). The loss would increase with the size of benefits. The average loss for all elderly families would be $260 (1.5 percent of average annual income).[64] Combining the COLA freeze with an increase in SSI benefits of $20 per month for individuals and $30 per month for families would significantly moderate the effect on the poor.[65] The CBO estimates that the COLA freeze would add 420,000 to the poverty population, 280,000 of whom would be elderly. Again, increases in SSI benefits would reduce the effect of the policy, limiting the addition to the poverty population to 300,000, among them 190,000 elderly.[66]

The discussion above indicates that the policy will affect the poor and the near poor among the elderly as well as those more able to bear the real income loss, but the loss would be limited to less than 3 percent of annual income on the average for the poor.

The COLAs and Recent Real Benefit Changes. Some opponents of COLA freezes note that social security recipients have recently suffered real income losses as a result of the six-month COLA delay in 1983. One estimate is that the delay will cost the average couple $1,698 by the end of the decade.[67] Supporters of the freeze argue that social security beneficiaries were overcompensated for changes in their cost of living in the late 1970s.

As noted above, the measure used to inflate benefits, the CPI, may not accurately capture changes in the cost of living of the elderly. In fact, the

CPI in general measures not changes in the cost of living but rather changes in the prices of a fixed market basket.[68] This measure has been criticized on a number of grounds, but in the late 1970s the homeownership component received particular attention. This component of the index is based on the actual expenditures of those purchasing homes at the time. It includes the full house price plus the interest cost for about fifteen years. Rising home prices and interest rates caused this component of the CPI to escalate rapidly in the late 1970s and to overestimate the change in the cost of homeownership for most homeowners.[69]

How has this flaw affected the beneficiaries of social security and the other retirement programs with COLAs? In July 1980 social security beneficiaries received a 14.3 percent COLA. Joseph J. Minarik estimated that if the COLA had been based on the personal consumption expenditure deflator, the increase would have been only 9.5 percent. The difference between the two indexes in this period was due primarily to their treatment of housing costs.[70] Since the elderly are not generally buying homes but rather live in already acquired housing, they benefited from the flaw in the CPI; that is, the real value of their benefits rose.[71]

THE GENEROSITY OF CIVIL SERVICE AND OTHER FEDERAL PENSIONS

Much of the discussion of issues above is not relevant to the question of freezing COLAs in the civil service, military, and other federal retirement programs. It is generally agreed that these programs belong in the unified budget since they are funded by general revenues. Further, as seen above, few of the recipients of these programs are poor or near poor. The issue here is one of the appropriate generosity of the pension programs and what has been promised to federal retirees.

On the one hand, opponents of freezing these COLAs argue that government workers and the military accepted their jobs in the belief that one of their benefits was a generous retirement program. For many civil servants, pay has been frozen by the upper limit on federal pay scales, and they have served the public at personal expense since their alternative opportunities offer higher pay. Generous pensions are viewed as their reward. This argument is most relevant to high-level civil servants and military retirees. In a sense, what is being argued is that real benefit protection has been promised to workers and that many civil servants have made career decisions based on this promise. Freezing or reducing the COLA protection would break this promise and might cause less able workers to be attracted in the future.

On the other hand, private pensions do not guarantee full inflation protection and in many cases provide very little, primarily because of the expense of such protection and the uncertainty it introduces into future pension liabilities. The federal government, because of its access to tax revenues, is able to provide full inflation protection. Supporters of freezing COLAs argue that federal retirees have fared better than other retirees (and than active federal workers) because of the COLAs and can afford a one-time freeze in the interests of budget reduction.[72]

EQUITY AMONG BENEFICIARIES

If a one-year freeze or other reduction in COLA payments is enacted, care must be taken to prevent the introduction of inequities into the social security system. If no change is made in the initial determination of benefits, which is based on a wage-indexed adjustment, an unintended notch may arise in the benefit structure; that is, recipients of slightly different ages with similar wage histories would receive different benefits. This difference would arise because social security benefits for those already retired are indexed to the CPI effective in December each year (and paid in January) and new retirees receive the wage-indexed adjustment in calculating their initial benefit (effective in January) but do not receive the COLA. Freezing one adjustment and not the other might cause benefit inequities, as workers who retire a few months apart with identical earnings records might receive different benefits.[73]

17

5

ALTERNATIVE PROPOSALS FOR CONSTRAINING COLAS

A myriad of possible policies would reduce benefits for social security and other federal pension programs and so help reduce the general budget deficit, but this section focuses exclusively on alternatives that deal with the COLA provisions of these programs.[74] These proposals are treated in two broad categories: those that affect all recipients and those targeted in such a way as to moderate the effect on poor or near poor beneficiaries.

ACROSS-THE-BOARD PROPOSALS

A Temporary Full COLA Freeze. This kind of policy eliminates the full COLA payment for one year or a limited number of years. The Senate proposal of a one-year freeze of COLA payments for all non-means-tested programs is an example of such a policy. As noted above, the CBO estimates that this policy would save $43.3 billion over the 1986–1990 period but would cause an additional 420,000 persons to become poor.[75]

The six-month delay of the July 1983 social security COLA was a variation on this theme. In addition, CPI increases between the first and third quarters of 1983 were ignored.[76] Thus, under both this and the proposed policy, future benefits are permanently reduced, yielding short-term and long-term savings.

Other variations on this theme delay COLAs to produce short-term benefits but do not permanently reduce benefits. One example would be to raise the trigger. Currently, the social security COLA is implemented only if inflation is above 3 percent. If a COLA is not granted, the next COLA would account for all inflation since the last COLA payment. The civil service and other retirement plans do not have such a trigger. Raising the social security trigger or introducing one in the other programs, particularly in a period of moderate inflation, could postpone COLA payments and produce short-term savings without permanently lowering future benefits. A similar result could be produced by putting COLA payments on a biennial schedule. One disadvantage of the schedule change is that since it is not linked to the inflation rate, it might create large real income losses if inflation were suddenly to escalate. Either of these policies could be implemented on a temporary or a permanent basis.

A Partial COLA. An alternative to a full COLA freeze or a delay of COLA benefits would be to modify the COLA formula so that it compensates recipients for only a portion of inflation. This could be a temporary or permanent change in the formula. Several kinds of partial COLAs have been discussed. One alternative provides recipients with an increase equal to the increase in the CPI minus some fixed percentage. The idea is that beneficiaries are not protected against the first x percent of inflation but are protected against any substantial loss of real income. The White House–Senate leadership proposal of a COLA equal to 2 percent plus the difference between the actual increase in the CPI and approximately 4 percent is of this form, since it is essentially a COLA equal to the CPI increase minus 2 percent. The CBO estimates that this proposal, if implemented for three years, would cause a 5.4 percent reduction in real benefits and an increase of approximately 600,000 in the poverty population.[77]

An alternative partial COLA would give recipients a payment equal to some fraction of the increase in the CPI, for example, 60 percent. This would reduce expenditures while protecting recipients against most real income loss during inflation. This is similar to the COLAs in many union wage contracts. Those workers, of course, also receive fixed wage increases, so that the COLA is not their only source of wage gains, as it would be for pension recipients. From the recipients' viewpoint, this kind of partial COLA, however, is probably preferable to a capped COLA, one that gives full inflation protection up to some maximum inflation rate, at least in periods of inflation uncertainty. The capped COLA would, of course, yield greater predictability for future expenditures (or at least narrow the range of forecasts) and thus create less budget uncertainty. Another possible partial COLA would compensate for inflation on a less than full year basis; for example, the COLA could be based on nine months rather than one year.

PROPOSALS CONCERNED WITH LOW-INCOME RECIPIENTS

As mentioned above, a prime concern of the opponents of a COLA freeze is the adverse effect of such a policy on the real income of poor and near poor beneficiaries. To address this concern, several alternatives have been proposed that are designed to moderate the effect on low-income recipients. One strategy is to combine a COLA freeze with increases in benefits under the Supplemental Security Income program, a federal means-tested program for the aged, blind, and disabled. Another possibility is to design a COLA reduction that exempts beneficiaries with low incomes. In either case, there is clearly a trade-off between protecting those with low incomes and deficit reductions. The proposals discussed in this section result in smaller budget reductions than those that are not concerned with low-income recipients.

COLA Reductions Combined with SSI Increases. The SSI program was established by the 1972 Social Security Amendments. It guarantees a minimum monthly income for the aged, blind, and disabled who qualify on the basis of assets and income. Since social security benefits are included in the income used to determine SSI benefits, a COLA increase in social security would reduce SSI benefits on a dollar-for-dollar basis. SSI benefits, however, are also indexed, so that a COLA increase would increase the net income of someone receiving both social security and SSI.[78]

The COLA freeze proposals discussed above exempt the SSI COLA from the freeze. Thus proposals that combine a COLA freeze or reduction with increases in SSI guarantee levels would increase the real income of SSI recipients. Both the Senate proposal and the White House–Senate leadership proposal include increases in the SSI guarantee level of $10 per month for individuals and $15 per month for couples.

These combined policies do have less adverse effect on the poor than policies that do not raise the SSI benefit, but it should be noted that the majority of elderly poor do not participate in the SSI program.[79] Therefore, these policies moderate but do not eliminate the effect of COLA reductions on the poor. The CBO estimates that the White House–Senate leadership combined COLA reduction and SSI benefit increase may lead to a situation in which 30 percent of elderly poor families and 15 percent of elderly near poor families would experience income gains. (For the nonelderly who receive benefits under the affected programs, the figures are 42 percent and 26 percent respectively.) These income gains among the poor and near poor clearly mitigate the increase in poverty resulting from the COLA freeze. Without the SSI increases the policy is estimated to result in 600,000 added poor. With the SSI increases, the figure becomes 530,000.[80]

In sum, use of the SSI program is one waa to reduce the effect of COLA freezes or reductions on those with low incomes. The strategy's main flaw is that the SSI beneficiary population does not include many poor and near poor who would be affected by the COLA reduction. Alternatives that aim directly at the low-income recipients of the programs with COLAs that are affected may be better targeted.

Proposals That Exempt the Poor. There are several ways to design COLA freezes or reductions that exempt the poor. One possibility is to enact a COLA freeze and exempt all those with benefits below the poverty threshold defined by the Bureau of the Census. This is fairly straightforward, but it has several drawbacks. First, benefits are not necessarily a good measure of income. Since benefits account for less than 40 percent of income for the elderly, some with low benefits may have higher incomes and be unnecessarily exempted. Second, this policy ignores assets and in-kind benefits. Neither the poverty threshold nor benefits take these into account. Finally, the policy entails some administrative expense in identifying those exempt from the freeze. A policy basing the exemption on total income rather than benefits and using assets would clearly be far more expensive administratively. The CBO forecasts that exempting recipients with benefits below the poverty threshold and limiting their COLA to an amount that would raise the benefit to the threshold would reduce budget savings due to a COLA freeze by $10 billion over the 1986–1990 period (from $43.3 billion to $33.1 billion). The policy would cause only 80,000 more poor, fewer than 50,000 over age sixty-five (rather than 420,000 total and 280,000 elderly without the exemption).[81]

A variation on this theme would exempt from the COLA freeze social security and railroad retirement benefits below the poverty threshold. In other words, the COLAs for these programs would be capped rather than eliminated. All beneficiaries would receive the COLA only on the part of their benefits that is below the poverty threshold. This is in essence a combination of the policy exempting benefits under the poverty threshold and a partial COLA for beneficiaries who have higher benefits. The budget savings would be considerably lower than under the last policy described. Total budget savings are estimated at only $16.5 billion over the 1986–1990 period. The increase in poverty due to this policy would be under 50,000. The 1986 budget savings from this policy are estimated at $2.5 billion, an across-the-board COLA freeze is estimated to yield $6.5 billion, and an exemption for beneficiaries with benefits below the poverty threshold is estimated to save $5.1 billion.[82]

Another strategy that could be used to reduce COLA payments while protecting the real value of benefits for low-income recipients would be to use the federal income tax system. That system is progressive, that is, tax liabilities as a percentage of income rise with income. Aged couples do not pay income tax if their adjusted gross income is below $7,400.[83]

Under the 1983 Social Security Amendments, one-half of social security benefits are taxable for individuals with income greater than $25,000 and families with income greater than $32,000.[84] Granting the full COLA but making it entirely taxable would reduce the after-tax net for some and exempt low-income recipients. For high-income recipients at most 50 percent would be taxed; for low-income recipients none would be taxed, and they would receive the full COLA. Such a policy would have the advantage of administrative ease and would give beneficiaries the promised protection of real before-tax income. They would then be subject to income taxes like the rest of the population.

In sum, a number of policies can be designed to moderate the effect of a COLA freeze or reduction on low-income recipients. All such policies achieve this goal at the expense of reduced budget savings.

NOTES TO TEXT

1. An exhaustive list of such programs is given in Congressional Research Service, *Indexation of Federal Programs*, 97th Congress, 1st session, May 1981, pp. 11–14.

2. Others include food stamps, school lunches, hospital and supplemental medical insurance, and medical assistance. These are described in ibid., pp. 11–14, and also in General Accounting Office, *An Analysis of the Effects of Indexing for Inflation on Federal Expenditures,* August 15, 1979, pp. 26–32.

3. Others in this category include the retirement programs of the Foreign Service, the Federal Reserve Board, the Comptroller General, the Central Intelligence Agency, and the Tennessee Valley Authority. See Congressional Research Service, *Indexation,* p. 11.

4. The Congressional Budget Office base-line 1985 projection includes outlays of $192 billion for social security and $23 billion for the civil service retirement program (the next highest). See Congressional Budget Office, "An Analysis of Selected Deficit Reduction Options Affecting the Elderly and Disabled," Staff Working Paper (March 1985), p. 6.

5. This section is based on material in Robert M. Ball, "Social Security Amendments of 1972: Summary and Legislative History," *Social Security Bulletin* (March 1973), pp. 12, 14.

6. Ibid., p. 14.

7. Ibid., p. 15.

8. Ibid.

9. Robert S. Kaplan, *Indexing Social Security: An Analysis of the Issues* (Washington, D.C.: American Enterprise Institute, 1977), p. 9.

10. Ibid.

11. John Snee and Mary Ross, "Social Security Amendments of 1977: Legislative History and Summary of Provisions," *Social Security Bulletin* (March 1978), p. 4.

12. Ibid., pp. 12–14.

13. The overindexation issue is discussed in Kaplan, *Indexing,* pp. 16–18; and in Alicia H. Munnell, *The Future of Social Security* (Washington, D.C.: Brookings Institution, 1977), pp. 30–38.

14. The actual computation is more complicated, and the benefit rate differs at different levels of wage-inflation-adjusted average monthly earnings.

15. See Snee and Ross, "Social Security Amendments," pp. 12–13.

16. A number of other changes in the social security system were made. For more information, see ibid., pp. 12–20.

17. Ibid., p. 12.

18. A. Haeworth Robertson, "Financial Status of Social Security Program after the Social Security Amendments of 1977," *Social Security Bulletin* (March 1978), p. 29.

19. The following description is based on John A. Svahn and Mary Ross, "Social Security Amendments of 1983: Legislative History and Summary of Provisions," *Social Security Bulletin* (July 1983), pp. 3–4.

20. Ibid., p. 5.

21. Ibid., p. 6.

22. Ibid., p. 7.

23. Ibid., p. 8.

24. The following description of the provisions is based on ibid., pp. 24–25.

25. Ibid., p. 41.

26. Congressional Research Service, *Indexation*, p. 199.

27. Ibid., pp. 199–200.

28. Ibid., p. 200.

29. Ibid.

30. Ibid., pp. 200–1.

31. Congressional Research Service, *Digest of Public General Bills and Resolutions*, 97th Congress, 2d session, pt. 1, pp. 16, 23, 117.

32. Congressional Research Service, *Digest of Public General Bills and Resolutions*, 98th Congress, 2d session, pt. 1, p. 115.

33. Congressional Research Service, *Indexation*, pp. 21–24. More detail is available in ibid., pp. 233–42.

34. Ibid., p. 31.

35. Ibid., p. 26.

36. Ibid., p. 27.

37. Office of Management and Budget, *Budget of the United States, Fiscal Year 1986*, February 1985, pp. 2–6.

38. In fact the COLA is specified as 2 percent plus the excess of actual inflation over the inflation projected by the Office of Management and Budget (OMB) at the

time. The OMB projections were 4.1 percent for 1986, 4.3 percent for 1987, and 4.1 percent for 1988. See *Bureau of National Affairs Daily Report for Executives* (hereafter cited as *BNA DER*), May 1, 1985, p. X-7; and Elizabeth Wehr, "FY '86 Budget Struggle Moves to Senate Floor," *Congressional Quarterly*, April 20, 1985, p. 723.

39. *BNA DER*, May 1, 1985, p. X-7.

40. *BNA DER*, April 16, 1985, p. X-6.

41. "Summary of the Senate's Fiscal 1986 Budget," *Congressional Quarterly*, May 18, 1985, p. 922.

42. Jacqueline Calmes, "House, with Little Difficulty, Passes '86 Budget Resolution," *Congressional Quarterly*, May 25, 1985, p. 971.

43. *BNA DER*, May 23, 1985, p. X-8.

44. Congressional Budget Office, "Analysis of Deficit Reduction Options," p. 22.

45. Svahn and Ross, "Social Security Amendments," p. 3.

46. Congressional Budget Office, "Analysis of Deficit Reduction Options," p. 41.

47. Robert J. Myers, "Investment Policies and Procedures of the Social Security Trust Funds," *Social Security Bulletin* (January 1982), pp. 3–4.

48. "Report of the National Commission on Social Security Reform," *Social Security Bulletin* (February 1983), p. 11.

49. Svahn and Ross, "Social Security Amendments," p. 30.

50. Henry C. Ballantyne, "Actuarial Status of the OASI and DI Trust Funds," *Social Security Bulletin* (May 1984), pp. 6–8.

51. Income taxes now paid on some social security benefits flow into the social security trust funds.

52. Bruce D. Schobel, "A Comparison of Social Security Taxes and Federal Incomes Taxes," *Social Security Bulletin* (July 1981), p. 30; and idem, "A Comparison of Social Security Taxes and Federal Income Taxes, 1980–1990," *Social Security Bulletin* (December 1981), p. 19.

53. Svahn and Ross, "Social Security Amendments," p. 28.

54. David Koitz, Congressional Research Service, "Constraining Social Security Cost-of-Living Adjustments, Background and Issues," January 1985, p. 1.

55. Based on CBO estimates for 1985. See Congressional Budget Office, "Analysis of Deficit Reduction Options," p. 6.

56. Council of Economic Advisers, *Economic Report of the President*, February 1985, p. 163.

57. Ibid., pp. 165, 174.

58. Ibid., p. 163.

59. Ibid.

60. Ibid., p. 164.

61. Ibid., p. 166.

62. Households include both families and unrelated individuals.

63. Congressional Budget Office, "Analysis of Deficit Reduction Options," p. 22.

64. Ibid., p. 49.

65. Ibid., p. 52.

66. Ibid., p. 58.

67. Edward R. Roybal, *Congressional Record*, January 24, 1985, p. E193.

68. For details on the construction of the CPI, see Phillip Cagan, "The Consumer Price Index as an Escalator of Social Security Benefits and Other Payments," in Colin D. Campbell ed., *Controlling the Cost of Social Security* (Washington, D.C.: American Enterprise Institute, 1984), pp. 207–32.

69. See ibid., pp. 214–17; and Joseph J. Minarik, "Does the Consumer Price Index Need Deflating?" *Taxing and Spending* (Summer 1980), pp. 17–24.

70. Minarik, "Does the CPI Need Deflating?" p. 17.

71. This effect has recently been reversed. Since 1983 and 1984 the CPI adjusted to reflect the rental value of housing (the CPI-X1) rose more rapidly than the CPI-W, used to inflate retirement benefits. See Koitz, "Constraining Social Security COLAs," p. 16.

72. For information on the controversy over civil service retirement indexation, see Congressional Research Service, *Indexation*, pp. 213–15. Information on the military retirement system may be found in American Enterprise Institute, "Military Retirement: The Administration's Plan and Related Proposals," July 1970.

73. Koitz, "Constraining Social Security COLAs," pp. 18–19.

74. Alternative policies are discussed in ibid., pp. 6–11; in Congressional Budget Office, "Analysis of Deficit Reduction Options"; and in Jonathan Rauch, "Congress Weighs Idea of Cuts in Social Security COLAs That Shield the Poor," *National Journal*, April 27, 1985, pp. 901–94. The following discussion draws on these three sources.

75. Congressional Budget Office, "Analysis of Deficit Reduction Options," pp. 41, 58.

76. Koitz, "Constraining Social Security COLAs," p. 29.

77. Richard Kasten and Ralph Smith, "Effects on Family Incomes of One Option for Reducing COLAs for Non-Means-Tested Program Benefits and Increasing SSI Benefits," Congressional Budget Office Memorandum, April 10, 1985. This estimate (like the other CBO estimates) is based on a simulation using data from the March 1984 Current Population Survey.

78. For information on SSI, see Congressional Research Service, *Indexation*, pp. 311–20.

79. Congressional Budget Office, "Analysis of Deficit Reduction Options," p. 23.

80. Kasten and Smith, "Effects on Family Incomes," pp. 4, 7.

81. Congressional Budget Office, "Analysis of Deficit Reduction Options," pp. 41, 58.

82. Ibid.

83. This is based on the 1984 standard deduction of $3,400 for a couple and four personal exemptions. The figure is $4,300 for a single individual.

84. Svahn and Ross, "Social Security Amendments," p. 26.

SELECTED AEI PUBLICATIONS

Regulation: The AEI Journal on Government and Society, published bimonthly (one year, $24; two years, $44; single copy, $5.00)

Broadcast Deregulation (1985, 33 pp., $3.95)

Review: 1984 Session of the Congress (1985, 76 pp., $4.95)

Proposed Procedures for a Limited Constitutional Convention (1984, 40 pp., $3.95)

Toxic Torts: Proposals for Compensating Victims of Hazardous Substances, (1984, 32 pp., $3.95)

Credit Controls: Should We Revive and Expand Them? (1984, 46 pp., $3.95)

Regulating Consumer Product Safety, W. Kip Viscusi (1984, 116 pp., cloth $14.95, paper $5.95)

Ethics-in-Government Laws: Are They Too "Ethical"? Alfred S. Neely IV (1984, 58 pp., $4.95)

The Regulation of Pharmaceuticals: Balancing the Benefits and Risks, Henry G. Grabowski and John M. Vernon (1983, 74 pp., $4.95)

• *Mail orders for publications to:* AMERICAN ENTERPRISE INSTITUTE, 1150 Seventeenth Street, N.W., Washington, D.C. 20036 • *For postage and handling, add 10 percent of total; minimum charge $2, maximum $10 (no charge on prepaid orders)* • *For information on orders, or to expedite service, call toll free 800-424-2873 (in Washington, D.C., 202-862-5869)* • *Prices subject to change without notice.* • *Payable in U.S. currency through U.S. banks only*

AEI ASSOCIATES PROGRAM

The American Enterprise Institute invites your participation in the competition of ideas through its AEI Associates Program. This program has two objectives: (1) to extend public familiarity with contemporary issues; and (2) to increase research on these issues and disseminate the results to policy makers, the academic community, journalists, and others who help shape public policies. The areas studied by AEI include Economic Policy, Education Policy, Energy Policy, Fiscal Policy, Government Regulation, Health Policy, International Programs, Legal Policy, National Defense Studies, Political and Social Processes, and Religion, Philosophy, and Public Policy. For the $49 annual fee, Associates receive

- a subscription to *Memorandum,* the newsletter on all AEI activities
- the AEI publications catalog and all supplements
- a 30 percent discount on all AEI books
- a 40 percent discount for certain seminars on key issues
- subscriptions to any two of the following publications: *Public Opinion,* a bimonthly magazine exploring trends and implications of public opinion on social and public policy questions; *Regulation,* a bimonthly journal examining all aspects of government regulation of society; and *AEI Economist,* a monthly newsletter analyzing current economic issues and evaluating future trends (or for all three publications, send an additional $12).

Call 202/862-6446 or write: AMERICAN ENTERPRISE INSTITUTE
1150 Seventeenth Street, N.W., Suite 301, Washington, D.C. 20036